This
Land Is
Your Land

This Land Is Your Land

The American Conservation Movement

by Sylvia Whitman

Lerner Publications Company • Minneapolis

To the Gleig sisters, Gaby and Jeanne —
two teachers who have planted so many seeds for the future

The following people deserve special thanks: Ed Allen, Bill Laing, Joe Linn, Walt Love, Damon Mackey, Ed Sincic, Roger Sweeney, Ernie Taylor — for their memories of the CCC; Linda Maraniss and Bill Partington — for their perspectives on conservation; Susan Breckner Rose — for her editing; and Mohamed Ben Jemaa — for his company.

Woody Guthrie: "The Great Dust Storm," words and music by Woody Guthrie, TRO © Copyright 1960, 1963 Ludlow Music, Inc., New York, NY, used by permission. Tom Lehrer: "Pollution," used by permission.

LIBRARY OF CONGRESS CATALOGING-IN-PUBLICATION DATA

Whitman, Sylvia, 1961–
    This land is your land : the American conservation movement / Sylvia Whitman.
        p.   cm.
    Includes bibliographical references (p. 84) and index.
    ISBN 0-8225-1729-9
    1. Environmental responsibility—United States—Juvenile literature. 2. Environmental protection—United States—Juvenile literature. 3. Conservation of natural resources—United States—Juvenile literature. 4. Yellowstone National Park—History—Juvenile literature. [1. Conservation of natural resources. 2. Environmental protection. 3. Environmental policy. 4. Yellowstone National Park. 5. Natural parks and reserves.]
I. Title.
GE195.7.W45   1994
363.7'00973—dc20
                                                          94–3099
                                                            CIP
                                                            AC

Manufactured in the United States of America
1 2 3 4 5 6 – I/JR – 99 98 97 96 95 94

Contents

Land Up for Grabs 6

Going, Going, Gone 18

Saving the Wilderness 34

The Dirty Thirties 50

Polluting the Planet 62

Making "Green" Routine 72

Bibliography 84

Index 86

LAND UP FOR GRABS

The waving to and fro of the gigantic fountain, when its jets are at their highest, and in a bright sunlight, affords a spectacle of wonder of which any description can give but a feeble idea. Our whole party were wild with enthusiasm.

—Lt. Gustavus Doane,
Yellowstone expedition report,
1870

By plane, train, bus, and car, more than two million people travel to Yellowstone National Park every year to watch the earth explode. This northwestern corner of Wyoming, a plateau of ancient volcanic lava, is a geologic pressure cooker. As rain seeps down through the ground, it comes into contact with gases or rocks heated by the planet's molten core. Trapped in cracks far below the surface, ferociously hot water turns into steam. The expanding steam pushes upward to escape, carrying with it anything in its path before erupting.

Thermal activity at Yellowstone takes many forms: geysers that rip skyward, hot springs that bubble over mineral deposits, and mud pots that splutter like simmering stews. Native Americans once described this cauldron as a place left unfinished by the Creator.

The United States annexed northwest Wyoming as part of the Louisiana Purchase in 1803, but almost 70 years passed before the government took note of Yellowstone. John Colter, a mountain man who had quit the Lewis and Clark expedition, happened upon the thermal water show while trapping in 1807. When he later bragged about his discovery back in St. Louis, no one paid much attention. Settlers in the city had heard too many tall tales, and they considered fur trappers especially unreliable. So they ignored reports from other scruffy traders and prospectors about "Colter's Hell," where a fisherman could catch a trout in one stream and boil it in another.

Rumors about this Wyoming wonderland did stir interest in the nearby territory of Montana, though. In August 1870, 19 respectable citizens—including an ex-governor—set out from Helena in search of Colter's Hell. Led by former Civil War general Henry Washburn, Montana's top surveyor, the group brought along two cooks to prepare the rations, packers to load the 40 horses and mules, and a dog. Lieutenant Gustavus Doane and a small cavalry detachment escorted the civilians in case of attack by Crow or Blackfoot Indians.

After nine days, the party reached the region of "yellow stone." They spent a month there, awed by a landscape hissing and howling as if filled with demons. "It is grand, gloomy, and terrible," wrote Doane, "a solitude peopled with fantastic ideas; an empire of shadows and gloom." Beyond the thermal pools, the lodgepole pine forest rustled with wildlife—moose, elk, bison, antelope, mink, coyote, wolf, bear, cougar, fox, as well as countless birds. The more the men explored, the more they marveled. They also christened their discoveries: Mount Washburn, for instance, and the geyser Old Faithful, which hurled more than 5,000 gallons of water into the air at almost hourly intervals. Sitting around the campfire, the men agreed that the federal government should preserve Yellowstone in its pristine state.

Once home, the explorers campaigned for a national park by writing articles and lecturing all over the country. The federal government responded to the publicity by granting Ferdinand Hayden $40,000 to organize a scientific expedition.

Head of the U.S. Geological Survey of the Territories, Hayden wanted visual documentation of his trip to Yellowstone. So he added photographer William Henry Jackson and painter Thomas Moran to his team of 34 men. The two artists turned out to be an inspired if unlikely combination. Jackson, who owned a studio in Omaha, Nebraska, was a hardy pioneer; Moran, who worked as an engraver in Philadelphia, was a frail romantic. Yet they worked well together.

In 1871, Hayden and his explorers traveled by wagon train from Utah north to Fort Ellis in Montana, then regrouped at a ranch in the

The members of the Hayden survey camp in Red Buttes in 1870. The hatless Ferdinand Hayden is seated at the far end of the table, and William Henry Jackson is standing on the right.

William Henry Jackson and his assistant, photographing in the Tetons in 1872

Yellowstone River valley. There they traded their clumsy wagons for nimble mules. Jackson loaded his animals with 400 pounds of photographic equipment. After following the river for three days, the party arrived at Mammoth Hot Springs. Water—at 160° Fahrenheit—cascaded over limestone terraces, shimmering like a rainbow. As the geologists gaped, Moran pulled out his watercolors.

For more than a month, Hayden's artists and scientists combed the area. In the field, Moran made sketches and helped Jackson set up his shots. Jackson processed his film along the way. He and a hired assistant washed photo plates in the hot springs—which sped up developing time. Later, painting on canvas back in his studio, Moran used Jackson's photos to refresh his memory.

Thomas Moran's painting entitled "Tower Falls and Sulphur Mountain, Yellowstone"

When Hayden returned to Washington at the end of the summer, he joined the members of Washburn's expedition in lobbying for a national park. He also enlisted the aid of the North Pacific Railroad, which was banking on trainloads of tourists buying tickets to Yellowstone.

More than any written report or commercial interest, however, art swayed the public and the politicians. For centuries, people had depended on painters to serve as eyewitnesses. Thomas Moran's watercolors conveyed Yellowstone's eerie grandeur. But the new medium of photography also fascinated Americans, who trusted the camera to tell the truth objectively. William Henry Jackson's black-and-white photos, with tiny humans posed beside Old Faithful foaming and erupting, proved beyond a doubt that this odd land existed.

In March 1872, President Ulysses S. Grant signed an act designating Yellowstone, an area larger than Rhode Island and Delaware combined, as the first national park:

> The tract of land in the Territories of Montana and Wyoming...is hereby reserved and withdrawn from settlement, occupancy, or sale under the laws of the United States, and dedicated and set apart as a public park or pleasuring ground for the benefit and enjoyment of the people.... Regulations shall provide for the preservation, from injury or spoilation, of all timber, mineral deposits, natural curiosities, or wonders within said park, and their retention in their natural condition.

William Henry Jackson's photograph entitled "Tower Falls 115 Feet"

MORE THAN ENOUGH FOR EVERYONE

Today, the creation of Yellowstone National Park sounds like a victory for environmentalists: A handful of citizens brought public pressure to bear on government, which spared more than two million acres of land from development. But in 1872, Americans weren't thinking in those terms.

The lobbyists for Yellowstone didn't constitute a political movement. They weren't crusading for wilderness preservation. Most wanted simply to protect the West's thermal curiosities. They hoped to stave off the tacky commercialism that had spoiled Niagara Falls in upstate New York. By 1871, according to novelist Henry James, Niagara Falls was "choked in the horribly vulgar shops and booths and catchpenny artifacts which have pushed and elbowed to within the very spray of the

By the 1870s, commercial development had sprawled to the edge of Niagara Falls.

falls." Hayden, an influential geologist, didn't like the idea of mineral-bath operators setting up shop on Yellowstone's hot springs.

The federal government could afford to be generous with land in the 1800s. The Louisiana Purchase had doubled the size of the United States at a cost of about $35 an acre. The United States soon acquired Florida, Texas, the Pacific Northwest, and the Southwest through wars, purchase, and squatting. Squatters played "finders keepers"; they settled in open territory and called it their own.

Throughout the 19th century, the General Land Office (later the Department of the Interior) sold public land at bargain prices. Railroads, mining companies, and timber barons benefited, but so did small farmers. The Land Act of 1804 allowed pioneers to buy 320-acre parcels for two dollars an acre. By giving away land, the Homestead Act—which took effect in 1863, during the Civil War—encouraged settlement of the West. For a small registration fee, any citizen over 21 could own 160 acres by living and working on the claim for five years. The federal government also granted territory to states. President Abraham Lincoln signed an 1864 bill assigning Yosemite Valley to California "for public use, resort, and recreation." Few people objected to the creation of the Yosemite reservation or to Yellowstone National Park eight years later. There was still plenty of land up for grabs.

PARADISE OF COD AND HONEY

Most Americans took such abundance for granted in 1872. It was the hallmark of the New World. The bears, the birds, the vast stretches of forest in North America amazed Europeans from the very first contacts. They raved about long-tailed passenger pigeons so numerous that they eclipsed the sun and white pines so tall they didn't need to be spliced together to serve as masts of sailing ships. Some explorers got carried away, claiming they had seen unicorns. Most Europeans, however, didn't need to exaggerate.

"The aboundance of Sea-fish are almost beyond beleeving," the Reverend Francis Higginson wrote of New England in 1630. Crossing

into Ohio and Indiana in 1797, the Reverend James Smith noticed that
"incredible numbers of bees have found their way to this delightful
region.... It is not an uncommon thing for people to take their wagon
and team and return loaded with honey." Each new territory disclosed
new natural riches, which inspired place names like Cape Cod.

The bounty dazzled newcomers, but settlers soon got down to
business. Like the Native Americans who had long lived on the East
Coast, colonists drew their livelihood from the land. Unlike the
Indians, however, the colonists altered it drastically. As early as 1642,
the Narragansett sachem (chief) Miantonomo noticed problems:

> Our fathers had plenty of deer and skins, our plains were
> full of deer, as also our woods, and of turkies and our coves
> full of fish and fowl. But these English having gotten our
> land, they with scythes cut down the grass, and with axes
> fell the trees; their cows and horses eat the grass and their
> hogs spoil our clam banks, and we shall all be starved.

Tribes differed in hunting and farming practices, but their lifestyle
minimized human impact on the environment. Native Americans
tended to move often, so the fields and woods that they abandoned
recovered. European immigrants, on the other hand, congregated in
permanent villages. Unlike the Indians—whom most whites dismissed
as "uncivilized savages"—settlers aimed to "improve" the countryside.
They cultivated single crops in the same plots until they had exhausted
the soil. Their cattle grazed until they had stripped off the natural
ground cover, opening the way for weeds. Linked by the Atlantic
Ocean to the markets of Europe, colonists removed from the land not
only what they needed, but what they could sell—excess crops, beavers
for hats, white oak for ships' planking.

The abundance of resources allowed settlers to be wasteful. They
built large houses of wood and heated them with cozy but inefficient
open fires. Carpenters used high-quality wood such as cedar for every-
day shingles, barrels, and fences. To save labor when clearing a field,
farmers cushioned the fall of a towering tree by cutting notches in
younger trees, which acted like collapsible shock absorbers. Many

farmers, in too much of a hurry to chop and haul the wood, burned the younger tree trunks beside the larger stumps. By the 1850s, as much as 75 percent of southern New England had been deforested, warming the climate and drying the soil as a result.

"FROM SEA TO SHINING SEA"

In 1832, the French politician Alexis de Tocqueville visited the United States. He analyzed the national character in his book *Democracy in America*:

> In Europe people talk a great deal of the wilds of America, but the Americans themselves never think about them; they are insensible to the wonders of inanimate nature and they may be said not to perceive the mighty forests that surround them till they fall beneath the hatchet. Their eyes are fixed upon another sight: the American people views its own march across these wilds, draining swamps, turning the course of rivers, peopling solitudes, and subduing nature.

In 1867, a wagon train crosses the Smoky Hill River in Kansas.

Although few 19th-century Americans read de Tocqueville, most would have considered his assessment high praise. They considered their energetic exploitation of resources to be "progress." Politicians made speeches about the country's "Manifest Destiny" to expand from the Atlantic Ocean to the Pacific. The march across the continent not only relieved crowding in seaboard cities, it revealed virgin forests, rich farmland, and mineral deposits to replace what earlier generations had stripped back East.

After the terrible suffering of the Civil War and the near-disbanding of the Union, the United States looked to the western territories to rejuvenate the country's sense of purpose. Many individuals, especially defeated Southerners, made fresh starts on the frontier. But even those Americans who didn't ride the wagon trains or the transcontinental railroad toward the sunset got a psychological boost just knowing the West was there.

Many easterners saw the Rocky Mountains and the Sierra Nevada through the eyes of painter Albert Bierstadt. At the New York Sanitary Fair of 1864, a fashionable benefit for Civil War aid, the German-American artist exhibited a panoramic view from his travels entitled *The Rocky Mountains—Lander's Peak.* Spectators carried or rented tiny tube telescopes to study the perfect details in the gigantic painting: leaves, rocks, birds. Critics hailed the majestic scenery and turned Bierstadt into a celebrity overnight. Soon, newly rich industrialists were paying over $10,000 a canvas for his western landscapes.

For the eastern elite, who had long aped sophisticated Europeans, these images began to cure a cultural inferiority complex. The upper classes had long been fighting to shed the stereotype that they were uncouth colonialists, as rough and primitive as the North American wilderness. Suddenly, the sublime paintings of Bierstadt and other artists gave them bragging rights. How could Europeans look down their noses at Americans when the Rocky Mountains and the Sierra Nevada surpassed the Swiss Alps in splendor?

The discovery of Yellowstone also fed national pride in the 1870s. Its strangeness bespoke the uniqueness of all the United States—as if

One of the most breathtaking vistas in the world — Yosemite Valley — photographed here in the 1850s

God had blessed this continent, and this country, beyond all others. By designating this remote tract as a public park, in a sense the federal government was placing Yellowstone in a frame and hanging it on a wall for everyone to admire. Public relations as well as preservation propelled the creation of the national park. But by saving a piece of wilderness *from* some of the people *for* all of the people, the Yellowstone act marked the beginning of a conservation ethic in the United States.

GOING, GOING, GONE

I can remember when the bison were so many that they could not be counted, but more and more Wasichus [white men] came to kill them until there were only heaps of bones scattered where they used to be.

The Wasichus did not kill them to eat; they killed them for the metal that makes them crazy, and they took only the hides to sell. Sometimes they did not even take the hides, only the tongues.... Sometimes they did not even take the tongues; they just killed and killed because they liked to do that....

And when there was nothing left but heaps of bones, the Wasichus came and gathered up even the bones and sold them.

—Black Elk,
Sioux medicine man, 1880s

In 1869, a mail train chugging across western Kansas screeched to a halt. Buffaloes, or bison, were crossing the track. Even the "iron horse," powered by a steam locomotive, could not plow through a wall of American bison. Weighing an average of 1,800 pounds, the bison was the largest animal in North America. For more than two hours, the engineer waited impatiently for the herd to pass.

In this instance, human beings and their machines backed down. But not for long. Industrial civilization and American wildlife were

18

heading on a collision course in the 19th century, and the shaggy brown bison became a symbolic casualty of a nation hell-bent on progress.

Colonists had killed off or driven west all the eastern bison by the early 1800s, when the United States began its rapid expansion. Because of immigration, the U.S. population leaped from 17 million people in 1840 to 32 million in 1860. Despite some hunting, bison roaming the Great Plains still outnumbered humans at least two to one in 1840.

Plains Indians—the Sioux, the Crow, the Blackfeet, the Comanche— all depended on bison. Native Americans believed bison emerged from a hole in the earth: Comanches passed down a tale of a medicine man disguised as a dog who barked until he scared the first herd out of the ground and on to the grasslands. Early Native American hunters stalked the beasts with lances or stampeded them off cliffs or into corrals. When white explorers and traders introduced guns and horses,

An 1895 photo of a Cheyenne camp. Women have prepared meat for drying on racks and cleaned and stuffed entrails as sausage (on rack at left).

Indians developed a risky, breathtaking chase. Women processed the kill—smoking meat for the winter and tanning hides for shields, clothes, and tepees. They used shoulder bones as hoes and turned bladders into canteens. Even though Native Americans believed the Great Spirit had blessed them with an unlimited supply of bison, they wasted nothing. They honored the holy gift.

But both the bison and the Plains Indian stood in the way of white settlement.

The transcontinental railroad—completed in 1869—cut right through the habitat of the great herds of bison. Rich European sportsmen traveled by train to the frontier, then set out with guides and plenty of champagne and guns to bag bison. In 1872, Grand Duke

Passengers and crew members of the Union Pacific Railroad eagerly join in shooting bison on the Great Plains.

Buffalo Bill Cody

Alexis of Russia rode in his private railroad car to rough-and-tumble Hays City, Kansas, where the U.S. cavalry served as his hunt guide.

For tourists on a budget in 1868, the Kansas and Pacific Railroad advertised a four-day, round-trip "buffalo excursion" for $10: "Buffaloes are so numerous along the road that they are shot from the cars nearly every day. On our last excursion our party killed twenty buffaloes in a hunt of six hours." Everyday travelers, most of whom carried guns, could also take potshots. One 1868 passenger reported:

> A shout "Buffalo crossing the track!" was heard and bang! bang! bang! simultaneously went several pieces.... The barrage wounded two of the buffalo; the locomotive whistled down brakes, and without waiting for the train to stop, everyone—passengers, engineer, conductor, brakeman— jumped off the cars and gave chase.

The railroads also made killing bison profitable for professional hunters. The Kansas and Pacific Railroad hired a 21-year-old former Pony Express rider named William Cody to provide meat for its construction crews. When he met up with a writer who churned out popular dime novels, William Cody was immortalized in print as Buffalo

Bill. Other crack shooters fed the army and supplied restaurants with steaks. They even shipped the meat on ice to St. Louis. But with bison meat selling for about a nickel a pound, butchering on site required a lot of work and wagon space for little profit. Many hunters simply abandoned carcasses to wolves after slicing off the tongue, which was then considered a delicacy. Preserved with salt, a tongue brought about 50 cents. Hides—which were tanned and sewn into warm and supple buffalo robes—turned into a hot commodity, too, worth between $2.00 and $3.50.

Innovations in easy-to-load firearms also doomed the bison. One rifle, the Sharps Big .50, enabled a hunter to fire from as far as 1,000 yards away from his target. As Indians observed, the gun "shoots today and kills tomorrow." J. Wright Mooar, one of two buffalo-hunting brothers from New England, downed more than 20,000 animals over a nine-year career.

Unofficially, army officers encouraged the hunters, even passing out ammunition. At the end of the 19th century, Native Americans were desperately defending what was left of their lands from miners,

Government agents distribute food rations to Sioux Indians. By the late 1800s, white settlers had wiped out the Indians' livelihood.

ranchers, homesteaders, and squatters. The U.S. government fought a series of Indian wars in the West with the goal of confining the tribes to tracts of land set aside as reservations. Strategists recognized that without bison to sustain them, native warriors would have to surrender. When Congress passed a bill "to prevent the useless slaughter of Buffaloes within the Territories of the United States" in 1874, President Grant, on the advice of his generals, refused to sign it.

Like poor farmers across the frontier, hungry Indians in the Dakotas gathered up skeletons from the buffalo slaughter and sold them for six dollars a ton. Freight trains carted the bones to factories in cities like St. Louis, where they were ground into fertilizer or china.

By 1900, only a few hundred bison survived in the wild.

A BIRD IN THE HAND

The lethal combination of wastefulness, weaponry, and greed endangered many other species besides bison. The 19th-century building boom in canals, roads, and railways allowed people to penetrate once-remote wilderness and to ship their kill to market.

Hunters targeted game birds like duck, woodcock, squab, and snipe to sell to wealthy gourmets in big cities like Boston, Chicago, and New York. Now country boys had an excuse to play hooky and wander through the woods with their dogs and their shotguns: Their good aim earned the family money. Professionals perfected new techniques in the mid-1800s, such as hiding in blinds or using live waterfowl as decoys. To catch the gregarious passenger pigeon, trappers tethered live pigeons to a stool (adding the term "stool pigeon" to the language) and netted hundreds of birds in a snap. People ate them, fed them to hogs, or melted them into oil for soap. Once, every newcomer to North America had gaped at the passenger pigeons that carpeted the sky in flocks more than a billion strong. By 1914, only one, named Martha, remained. She died that year in a Cincinnati zoo.

Fashion took its toll on several species. To be in style, ladies pinched their waists with whalebone corsets and draped their wide skirts over whalebone hoops. If men's beaver hats had not passed out of style in

In the late 1800s, women wore the feathers of exotic birds on their hats and whalebone corsets around their waists.

the 1840s, trappers probably would have skinned beavers into extinction. Feathers—and whole, stuffed songbirds—came into vogue as decoration on women's hats and gowns. On two strolls through Manhattan in 1896, an ornithologist noted that 542 out of the 700 women on his route were wearing feathered bonnets. Their finery represented more than 40 varieties of birds, from Acadian owls to pileated woodpeckers.

Exotic wading birds, such as pink flamingos, suffered most. When Civil War deserters fled into Florida, they discovered the Everglades, where great blue herons and snowy white egrets roosted in dense mangrove swamps. Soon the ex-soldiers were supplying feathers to hat makers in New York. Milliners paid $32 an ounce—about twice the price of gold—for egret plumes.

The American Ornithologist Union estimated that five million North American birds died for adornment in 1886.

Because of the capitalist formula of supply and demand, bison and heath hens increased in value as they declined in numbers. But human activity also compromised wildlife in more subtle ways. Cutting down trees and plowing up prairies destroyed habitat. Museums stuffed animals in the name of science. And well-meaning travelers sometimes imported foreign species that overwhelmed native ones—like English sparrows who stole the nests out from under American bluebirds.

SURVEYORS WITH A SCIENTIFIC EYE

Such massive changes in the environment did not go unnoticed. Some citizens began to question the recklessness of "progress" in the United States. Slowly, three broad groups—scientists, romantic philosophers, and sportsmen—began to voice their concerns.

Charles Darwin's theory of evolution, set forth in *The Origin of Species* (1859), rocked Europe and the United States. For centuries, Europeans had looked upon the world as a finished product of God's creation. According to Biblical tradition, God made "man" in His image and gave him "dominion" over the beasts of the field. Darwin's theory that all species, including *homo sapiens*, or humans, had developed over time suggested that forces other than God were constantly reshaping the world. That idea alarmed many religious leaders, but it also challenged scientists to look at the natural world in a new way.

In the late 19th century, science was coming into its own as a profession, with higher standards of education and more specialization. In 1882, the American Association for the Advancement of Science split Natural History into nine categories with multiple subdivisions that covered everything from botany to zoology. Natural historians began to study ecology—the relationships of living creatures to each other and to their surroundings.

Massachusetts chemist Ellen Swallow Richards helped popularize the field of ecology. A graduate of Vasser College and in 1871 the first woman to enter the Massachusetts Institute of Technology, Richards linked human health to the quality of the environment. She designed a lab to test water and traveled all over the world analyzing samples. Her research prompted Massachusetts to establish the first standards for drinking water in the United States.

Another early ecologist was Stephen A. Forbes. The son of an Illinois farmer, Forbes left the cavalry after the Civil War to pioneer limnology, the study of bodies of fresh water. For his book *The Lake as Microcosm* (1887), he analyzed stomach contents of lake birds to find out what they ate and concluded that they kept the bug population in check. Later, as head of the U.S. Bureau of Entomology, he noted that many of the destructive insects in the United States—such as the cotton-devouring boll weevil—originated overseas. He took the next step and tried to import the bugs' enemies as natural pesticides.

Linking birds to the success of agriculture saved their skins. In 1883, ornithologists established a professional society and convinced the federal government to found the Division of Economic Ornithology to explore the connection between birds and mammals. That agency evolved into the Division of Biological Survey in 1890 and eventually became the U.S. Fish and Wildlife Service.

The Biological Survey and the Geological Survey gave the federal government the first thorough inventory of its natural resources. An explorer as well as a teacher and a geologist, Major John Wesley Powell mapped much of the West. Surgeons had amputated his wounded right arm after the Civil War battle of Shiloh, but Powell remained, in the words of a friend, "a gallant leader." In the 1860s and 1870s, his adventurous expeditions made newspaper headlines, especially his death-defying boat ride through the Grand Canyon on the rapids of the Colorado River.

A photo of Rio Virgin, Utah, taken in the 1870s on one of John Wesley Powell's surveys

John Wesley Powell's survey crew loads the boats on the Colorado River.

Much as Congress appreciated Powell's surveys, it did not always listen to his advice. In his 1878 *Report on the Lands of the Arid Region of the United States*, Powell warned that farmers would have to cooperate and innovate in the West because of a scarcity of water. However, many Americans believed that almost magically "rain followed the plow"—even into the desert. Nonetheless, Powell spurred U.S. leaders to think about managing the country's growth.

VISITORS IN CIVILIZED LIFE

While scientists were appealing to reason, romantics were arguing from emotion. Through their writings, two 19th-century nature philosophers gave voice to a growing discontent with materialistic society.

Henry David Thoreau spoke from the East. Born and raised in Concord, Massachusetts, he came from an old Yankee family. After graduating from Harvard College, he returned home to write, mostly in the form of journals. In 1845, at the age of 28, Thoreau chopped down a pine tree and built a hut beside Walden Pond, where he lived alone for two years and two months.

He recalled that experience in *Walden* (1854), a memoir and meditation. In the book, he contrasted the tranquility of the woods with the bustle of commerce encroaching upon Walden—the train whistling past town every day, the laborers cutting peat from the bog and ice from the pond to sell. As Thoreau tended his beans, he wondered why people longed for luxury when it seemed to enslave them.

Thoreau advised his readers to "simplify, simplify." He found in his physical poverty at Walden a spiritual richness. Although he admitted feeling lonely at first, he discovered during a rainstorm the "sweet and beneficent society of Nature, in the very pattering of the drops, and in every sound and sight around my house, an infinite and unaccountable friendliness."

Thoreau called himself "a sojourner in civilized life." "In wildness," he said, "is the preservation of the world."

In the West, John Muir echoed this search for integrity in nature. While Thoreau plumbed the deep waters of a Massachusetts lake, Muir scanned the high peaks of the Sierra Nevada of California. "Yosemite," he wrote, "is the grandest, most divine of all earthly living places, the Lord's mountain house."

Born in Scotland and raised on a Wisconsin farm, Muir left the University of Wisconsin for Canada in 1864. After the Civil War, he returned to Indianapolis and worked in a factory, until he accidentally stabbed his eye with a metal file. When he recovered his sight, he hiked 1,000 miles to the Gulf of Mexico and then headed west on a ship to California. In 1868, at age 30, he hiked into Yosemite Valley. His heart never left.

Muir herded sheep in the area, then ran a sawmill. After he married the daughter of a doctor who raised grapes and pears, he tended the orchards. Whenever Muir could, though, he tramped into the wilds. He traveled without much gear, sleeping on pine boughs and living on tea and oatmeal. Some locals thought this wiry, bearded outdoorsman a bit loony.

Using quill pens made from eagle feathers he had found, Muir wrote about the Sierra Nevada—first in his journals, then for *Scribner's Monthly* in the 1870s. Eastern readers responded to his passion. With horror, he described the mighty sequoias falling to the loggers' saws.

"The Three Brothers" in Yosemite Valley, California

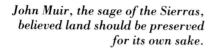

John Muir, the sage of the Sierras, believed land should be preserved for its own sake.

He blamed ranchers' sheep for nibbling away the undergrowth and exposing the hillsides to wind and water erosion.

In the early 1880s, Muir helped draft legislation to enlarge Yosemite. Opponents squashed the bill. But the pen proved mightier than the political interest groups. In 1889, Robert Underwood Johnson, an editor at *Century* magazine, visited Muir to solicit some articles. After a tour through Yosemite, Johnson and Muir decided to work for the creation of Yosemite National Park. Armed with Muir's eyewitness accounts in *Century*, Johnson lobbied hard for the park, which President Benjamin Harrison signed into existence in October 1890.

Eccentric John Muir had emerged as the sage of the Sierras.

"MANLY SPORT WITH A RIFLE"

Sportsmen formed the third leg of the unlikely triad of 19th-century conservationists. In the colonial period, most men hunted to put meat on the family table. As manufacturing transformed the United States from an agricultural to an industrial nation in the 19th century, cities grew. Laborers putting in 12-hour shifts in coal mines, cotton mills, or shoe factories bought the ingredients for supper at the market. But investors profiting from industry had time and money on their hands. They hunted for fun.

Clubs in places like Maryland's Chesapeake Bay and New York's Adirondack Mountains catered to this leisure class. The clubs provided guides and dogs, as well as plenty of servants to run baths and cook up elk or goose at the end of a day.

But society shooters ran into competition from commercial hunters who made a living with their guns. The conflict pitted upper class against lower class, playboys against working stiffs. At first, sportsmen simply bought up hunting grounds, but locals ignored the No Trespassing signs. Worried that commercial hunters were wiping out game, the amateurs banded together to take action.

Founded in 1844, the New York Sportsmen's Club led the charge by introducing laws that limited the open season on birds such as quail and grouse. Many states already had such game laws on the books, some of which predated the American Revolution. In 1639, Rhode Island had prohibited deer hunting for six months of the year to guarantee a steady supply of venison. But in the 19th century, these laws were rarely enforced. Citizens who tried to end poaching faced opposition from railroads, hotels, and merchants who profited from illegal hunting.

Inactive during the Civil War, sportsmen's associations multiplied in the 1870s to more than 300. New magazines, such as *Forest and Stream*, editorialized in favor of conservation.

Typical of these concerned sportsmen was a young New York legislator named Theodore Roosevelt. An amateur naturalist, he published more than a dozen books of natural history. But like the famous bird painter John James Audubon, he did his collecting with a gun. He killed, mounted, and studied his specimens.

In the 1880s, Roosevelt vacationed in the Dakota Badlands to shoot bison. The frontier so appealed to him that he invested more than $40,000, a third of his inheritance, in a cattle ranch. He was an absentee cowboy until 1884, when his mother and his beloved wife,

Theodore Roosevelt in the Badlands

Alice, died within hours of each other. The 26-year-old assemblyman withdrew from politics and returned to the Badlands. For the next two years, he rounded up steers, brought down grizzlies, and even knocked out a drunk in a saloon who called him "four eyes." Cowboys joked about Roosevelt's aristocratic speech and buckskin suit, but they admired his energy and his feeling for the West. As he wrote to his sister, "The country is growing on me, more and more."

As a rancher, Roosevelt witnessed the West's problems, including the butchery of bison and bighorn sheep. After he returned to New York, he established the Boone and Crockett Club in 1887 "to promote manly sport with the rifle" and "to work for the preservation of large game" through legislation and study. He limited membership to about 150 bigwigs—including painter Albert Bierstadt, Civil War general William Tecumseh Sherman, and Senator Henry Cabot Lodge. When Teddy Roosevelt assumed the presidency of the United States in 1901, conservation moved to the top of the national agenda.

SAVING THE WILDERNESS

It would be utterly wrong to allow a few individuals to exhaust for their own temporary personal profit the resources which ought to be developed through use so as to be conserved for the common advantage of the people as a whole.
—President Theodore Roosevelt, address to Congress, 1907

V ice President Theodore Roosevelt was hobnobbing at a Fish and Game League outing at Lake Champlain, New York, when news reached him of a national crisis. An assassin had shot President William McKinley twice; a button deflected one bullet, but the other tore through his abdomen.

Roosevelt rushed to McKinley's bedside in Buffalo. Within a few days, doctors declared that the president would recover. To reassure the nation, Roosevelt joined his second wife and six children on vacation at a club in the Adirondack Mountains. On September 13, 1901,

34

he and his oldest sons were hiking down Mount Marcy when a messenger met them on the trail with a telegram: "The President appears to be dying." The clubhouse had no phone. At 11:00 P.M., Roosevelt boarded a buckboard for the rough, 50-mile ride to the station, where a train was waiting to whisk him to Buffalo. By then McKinley had died. The next afternoon, Roosevelt, 43, took the oath of office.

"I told McKinley it was a mistake to nominate that wild man," complained one fellow Republican. "Now look—that damned cowboy is president of the United States!"

For the next seven years, Roosevelt preached environmental reform from the bully pulpit of the White House. In 1896, the Supreme Court had ruled that wildlife belonged to the state, not to people who owned the land underfoot, and this decision had given a boost to advocates of game laws. Roosevelt supported local efforts to stop illegal hunting

*Opposite: **Governor Theodore
Roosevelt hunting.**
Right: **President Theodore
Roosevelt and John Muir at Glacier
Point, Yosemite Valley,
in May 1903***

The Grand Canyon of the Colorado River, Arizona, in the 1870s. Note the person seated at the upper left of the photo.

and broadened federal protections for wildlife. In 1900, Congress had passed the Lacy Act, which outlawed interstate commerce in poached meat, fur, or feathers. Roosevelt pressed for enforcement. As New York Zoo director William Hornaday said, the president "gave the vanishing birds and animals the benefit of every doubt."

Roosevelt also took bold initiatives. He wrangled through Congress the Reclamation Act of 1902, which implemented some of John Wesley Powell's ideas about irrigating the West. In 1903, Roosevelt issued an executive order setting aside Pelican Island in Florida as the first federal bird reservation. He also used his power to set aside national monuments—only Congress could designate national parks—to put the Grand Canyon off-limits to developers in 1908.

Not everyone agreed with Roosevelt's agenda, especially businessmen who benefited from easy access to the lumber, minerals, and grass on public land. But Roosevelt easily won election to a second term in 1904, and politicians liked to side with a winner.

THE BAKED-APPLE CLUB

As Gifford Pinchot, Roosevelt's right-hand aide, wrote in 1910, conservation

> stands against the waste of the natural resources which cannot be renewed, such as coal and iron; it stands for the perpetuation of the resources which can be renewed, such as the food-producing soils and the forests; and most of all it stands for an equal opportunity for every American citizen to get his fair share of benefit from these resources, both now and hereafter.

Unlike John Muir, Pinchot did not believe in preserving land for its own sake. He shaped conservation in the practical image of professional forestry, for the use of the people.

As their woodlands fell to the ax, Europeans had pioneered the science of forestry. German immigrants, among them Carl Schurz, the first U.S. secretary of the interior, introduced forestry to the United States. At first, Americans had to travel abroad to study fire control, replanting, and other techniques that kept the supply of timber steady. Gifford Pinchot trained in France. When he returned to the United States, he first worked for the Vanderbilt family on their vast North Carolina estate.

Pinchot already headed the U.S. Bureau of Forestry when Roosevelt took office. But Pinchot's friendship with the president magnified his influence. They hunted together as Boone and Crockett Club members. One day, after the two had tramped through the swamps of Washington's Potomac River, a servant caught Pinchot wiping his wet sleeve on a post by the stairs. She "pointed her finger at me in reproof," Pinchot wrote, "and exclaimed, 'You've been out with that president!'"

In 1905, Roosevelt transferred the administration of federal woodlands to a "Forest Service" under Pinchot's control. Pinchot recruited an eager crew from new forestry programs at universities such as Yale and Michigan State. Although Pinchot approved of *using* land, he raised fees for mining permits and limited grazing in the spring so natural grasses could reseed themselves. In the early days of the Forest

Lumberjacks at work in Michigan in 1892. Pinchot believed in the regulated use of land, including lumbering.

Service, staffers gathered at Pinchot's home in the evening to talk conservation with visitors, members of Congress, even the president. They dubbed themselves the Baked-Apple Club in honor of the refreshments made by Pinchot's mother.

Regulation of economic activities such as mining and ranching aroused resistance, especially in the West. In 1907, senators tacked on an amendment blocking the creation of new national forests to a funding bill. Expecting Congress to override a veto, Roosevelt decided not to protest. But first, he and Pinchot pulled a fast one. Poring over maps, Forest Service officials identified 16 million acres that the president could easily add to existing forests. In 10 days, Roosevelt issued 33 proclamations expanding national forests. Then he signed the bill that took away his authority.

FOLLOW THE LEADER

As the conservation president, Roosevelt preserved 18 national monuments, 51 national wildlife refuges, and 130 million acres of national forest for future Americans. Just as importantly, he showed his fellow citizens how to enjoy them.

He made roughing it a lifelong hobby. In Washington, he hiked through Rock Creek Park, carrying a gun for protection since his Secret Service officers couldn't always keep up with him. Journalists tagged along on the president's many out-of-town hunting expeditions. In 1902, he was stalking Louisiana black bear—with no luck—when his host trapped a cub. Roosevelt refused to shoot it. A cartoon in the *Washington Post* and articles across the country contrasted Roosevelt's tough talk with his kind heart. When a Brooklyn store owner christened his wife's cuddly stuffed animals teddy bears, they became as popular as the president.

The public knew that Roosevelt had plunged into outdoor recreation to improve his health. He had been a sickly child, nearsighted and asthmatic, and bullies had picked on him. Riding, rowing, hiking, and camping strengthened his body. They also sharpened his mind and toughened his moral fiber, Roosevelt believed. In his *Autobiography*

John Muir shows Teddy Roosevelt through Yosemite National Park.
"I wouldn't miss this for anything," shouted Roosevelt. "This is bully!
Hurrah for Yosemite!"

(1913), he reminisced about his stint as a rancher in the Dakota Badlands: "It was a fine, healthy life, too; it taught a man self-reliance, hardihood, and the value of instant decision."

At the turn of the century, many Americans shared that nostalgia about the Wild West. In 1893, University of Wisconsin professor Frederick Jackson Turner presented a paper to the American Historical Association declaring, "the frontier has gone." Turner argued that confronting the wilderness had molded national character. A European might think Americans coarse, but they met challenges with curiosity, inventiveness, and plenty of energy. The taming of the West, wrote Turner, "has closed the first period of American history."

Although ordinary citizens didn't read history journals, they knew that the United States had reached a milestone. Everything was moving, changing, so fast. Easterners had learned from newspapers, magazines, and word of mouth about the West. Even as they applauded the advance of civilization, Americans also felt a profound loss.

Popular artists pulled heartstrings. In *The Last of the Buffalo* (1888), Albert Bierstadt painted a lone Indian spearing a mighty bison on a plain littered with skulls. City residents in the United States and Europe—even Queen Victoria—flocked to Buffalo Bill's Wild West Show to catch a final glimpse of a simulated Pawnee Indian war dance or a tethered antelope. Pride and sadness at the passing of the frontier lasted well into the 20th century, fueled by movie Westerns.

With change came worry. In 1830, 1 out of 15 Americans lived in a city with more than 8,000 people; by 1900, 5 out of 15 did. Overcrowding and open sewers in big cities spawned epidemics of cholera and dysentery. Factories spewed black smoke into the air and foul sludge into the water. Like Turner, many Americans traced their vigor and can-do spirit to the farm and the frontier. They wondered what sort of citizen an industrial society would produce.

Men and women complained of headaches and malaise from the stress of urban life. Industrialists who sat at desks all day feared they were going soft. Like Teddy Roosevelt, those who could afford to leave town headed for the country.

CALL OF THE WILD

Reporting for the *Atlantic Monthly* in 1898, John Muir noted:

> The tendency nowadays to wander in wildernesses is delightful to see. Thousands of tired, nerve-shaken, overcivilized people are beginning to find out that going to the mountains is going home; that wildness is a necessity; and that mountain parks and reservations are useful not only as fountains of timber and irrigating rivers, but as fountains of life.

Six years earlier, Muir and 26 other Californians had gathered in a lawyer's office to found the Sierra Club, dedicated to both conservation and recreation. The club sponsored outings for members and friends, including an annual high trip to the mountains. Countless books and articles encouraged this outdoorsy trend. "The wilderness hath charms," wrote George S. Evans for *Overland Monthly* magazine in 1904. "It will give you good red blood; it will turn you from a weakling into a man."

Joseph Knowles, a part-time illustrator, staged a publicity stunt to capitalize on the cult of the wild. On August 4, 1913, he summoned reporters to watch him disappear, naked, into the Maine woods. From time to time, he left birch-bark letters under a stump. After he emerged in October, a crowd of 20,000 in Boston clambered to hear him speak about how he survived—killing a bear for its coat, lighting a fire with sticks. Even though critics tracked down evidence that he had actually stayed in a cabin, fans bought 300,000 copies of his book *Alone in the Wilderness*.

Unlike most men, most women of the early 20th century didn't go anywhere alone—especially into the woods. But the health benefits of recreation encouraged many women to accompany their husbands and brothers. Early Sierra Club photos show women, including John Muir's two daughters, in sturdy boots and hats on Yosemite outings. Since the mid-1800s, reformers and feminists had been preaching exercise and the end to lung-crushing corsets—if only to improve fitness for motherhood. Amelia Jenks Bloomer urged women to trade long skirts for loose trousers, although bloomers never gained much of a following. But as respectable women joined the bicycling craze of the 1890s and took up other sports for their health, they began to wear less restrictive clothing and lead less restrictive lives.

Reformers started programs to introduce kids to wholesome outdoor activities. In 1877, rich New Yorkers founded the Fresh Air Fund, which sent inner-city youngsters away from crime-ridden tenements to a Pennsylvania farm and to summer camps. Middle-class boys joined the Boy Scouts. War hero Sir Robert Baden-Powell mustered the first

Scout leaders give a Boy Scout a cooking test in 1919.

troop in England, and scouting gained instant acceptance in the United States. Nature writer Ernest Thompson Seton published the first Boy Scout handbook in 1910—promoting woodcraft "to combat the system that has turned a large proportion of our robust, manly, self-reliant boyhood into a lot of flat-chested cigarette smokers."

Juliette "Daisy" Gordon Low—a well-born Southerner and a friend of Baden-Powell—organized the Girl Guides, and soon changed the name to Girl Scouts. Like the educators who founded the Camp Fire Girls in 1910, Low had to reassure parents that a little dirt wouldn't destroy a girl's femininity. As *Literary Digest* reported in 1924:

> Anxious families wonder, "Can she shoulder responsibilities after the glorious independence out of doors?" ... "Can she cook?" asks the man. "Can she sew? Can she take care of sick people? Can she save money out of a picayune income? Or will she bust right out in the middle of some jam, to go off and be a Daisy Crockett?"

Girl Scouts boating in 1912

Girl Scouts building a fire

To soothe critics, Girl Scouts' uniforms were soon changed from tights and bloomers to skirts. But thanks to the support of high-society matrons, Low convinced the public that girl scouting bred "the best sort of mother, sister, sweetheart, and friend of the future."

THE PEOPLE'S PARKS

National parks beckoned to nature converts. But not all guests knew how to behave. When the secretary of war visited Yellowstone in 1875, he found antlers from more than 4,000 elks slaughtered by poachers the previous winter. Vandals had written their names on the walls of the pools. One woman was caught with an ax poised to hack off a geyser cone. In 1886, the government finally sent in the cavalry to stop vandalism.

But even with military assistance, local administrators of far-flung national parks did not have enough money or people to manage them well. One wealthy Chicago salesman, Stephen Mather, complained in a letter to his friend Franklin Lane, the secretary of the interior. Lane wrote back, "If you don't like the way the national parks are being run, come on down to Washington and run them yourself."

A group of people (lower left) *hike on Comanche Trail in Bryce Canyon National Park.*

So Mather accepted a job as Lane's assistant. With his own fortune, he organized free trips for influential businesspeople, editors, and politicians. Comforts on the trail included air mattresses, white linen tablecloths, and freshly baked bread. Thanks to his lobbying, Congress established the National Park Service (NPS) in 1916.

As director of the NPS, Mather continued to wine and dine bigwigs. Sometimes he drove them around in his Packard touring car. He also welcomed tourists. Public support for parks helped him coax money from Congress.

During World War I, from 1914 to 1919, Americans who once vacationed in Europe stayed home, motoring across the country in newfangled automobiles. In 1910, there were 458,000 cars on the road; in 1925, there were more than 17 million. Mather pushed for highway construction near parks. He also introduced educational programs for tourists, hiring both male and female rangers to teach them.

On a Sunday morning in 1922, campers begin their day in Lake Basin Public Camp, Cleveland National Forest, California.

A carload of people travel the overland auto route in Sequoia National Park in 1908.

Nature preserves no longer belonged to the elite. Some purists resented the masses of people who tossed litter from cars. "They own as much of the parks as anybody else," Mather once answered. "We can pick up the tin cans. It's a cheap way to make better citizens."

BUSINESS AS USUAL

Conservation suffered setbacks in the two decades after Teddy Roosevelt left office. The Hetch Hetchy standoff in 1913 divided the movement. Back at the turn of the century, the growing city of San Francisco proposed damming and flooding the Hetch Hetchy Valley in Yosemite National Park to form a reservoir. At first, the federal government said no. Fires had long plagued San Francisco, but the fire

John Muir led the fight to save the lovely Hetch Hetchy Valley.

that followed the terrible earthquake of 1906 dramatized the city's water crisis. One man had to use 80,000 gallons of vinegar to save a burning building. Pro-dam forces argued that Yosemite already had one lovely valley and San Francisco needed cheap water. They enlisted Gifford Pinchot, a believer in the "wise use" of nature to benefit people. Anti-dam activists protested that the city could find water elsewhere and no one should disturb a national park. John Muir lobbied hard for leaving Hetch Hetchy alone. Commercial interests, he wrote, "seem to have a perfect contempt for Nature, and instead of lifting their eyes to the God of the mountains, lift them to the Almighty Dollar."

Muir and the Sierra Club engaged the public in the battle. But even with the media outside San Francisco on their side, the dam bill passed in 1913. Very disappointed, Muir died a year later at age 76. Although builders had promised a sparkling lake for recreation as well as a water supply, Hetch Hetchy reservoir ended up an ugly scab on the national park system.

But Hetch Hetchy Valley was dammed to form a reservoir.

Gifford Pinchot faced his own difficulties. Although he remained in charge of the Forest Service under Roosevelt's successor, Pinchot criticized the secretary of the interior, his boss, about coal leases in Alaska. He soon lost his job.

Through the pro-business 1920s, lumberers, ranchers, and miners exerted even more influence over the Department of the Interior, custodian of the country's natural resources. The Teapot Dome scandal exposed that cozy relationship. In 1921, President Warren G. Harding transferred control of some navy oil reserves to his secretary of the interior, Albert Bacon Fall. Fall then leased the fields in Teapot Dome, Wyoming, to an oil operator. The Senate investigated suspicious deals between Fall and the oil operator, and in 1929, a court convicted Fall of accepting bribes. But by then the public had lost interest in Teapot Dome. On October 24, 1929, "Black Thursday," the New York stock market plunged so fast that a few despairing brokers dove to their deaths from office windows.

The Great Depression had begun with a crash.

THE DIRTY THIRTIES

It fell across our city
*   like a curtain*
*   of black rolled down.*
We thought it was our judgment;
We thought it was our doom.
    —folk singer Woody Guthrie,
"The Great Dust Storm," 1930s

An ill wind blew across the Great Plains in the mid-1930s. Drought, scorching heat, and unwise farming practices had stripped the ground cover. Every breeze stirred the cracked, dry earth, and heavy winds whipped up frightening "black blizzards." By 1936, erosion had destroyed 9 million acres and damaged another 80 million in the Texas panhandle, western Oklahoma, Kansas, Nebraska, eastern Colorado, and parts of Wyoming, Montana, and the Dakotas. Writers christened the area the Dust Bowl.

Looking back decades later, politician Stewart Udall called the Dust Bowl "a bill collector sent by nature." In the 1880s, cattle ranchers had scorned "sod busters," farmers who settled the plains and broke ground with their plows. Despite periodic dry spells, though, the land yielded generously. When Europe turned to the United States for wheat during World War I, the U.S. government spurred production by guaranteeing farmers a princely two dollars a bushel. Instead of alternating crops and leaving some fields fallow, or unused, families put all their acres into wheat. That exhausted the soil. Plains farmers spent their war earnings on machines fresh off the assembly line: cars, tractors, and combines to harvest and thresh grain. Motors replaced horses. Speculators—suitcase farmers—with no ties to the land took up agriculture for profit. Once mechanized, farmers planted faster and more often. They believed they were helping the soil hold rain. In fact, they were uprooting grasses that protected land from wind and water erosion.

In 1931, a seven-year drought began on the Great Plains. Air currents swept the dry dirt beyond the prairie, darkening the skies of Boston, New York, Washington, and Atlanta. In May 1934, 12 million tons of topsoil from Montana and the Dakotas settled on Chicago like volcanic ash. In Kansas the next year, a seven-year-old boy suffocated in a drift, and Red Cross volunteers passed out face masks to prevent

A farmer harvests wheat near Carlsbad, New Mexico, in June 1916.

Dust piles up by farm buildings in South Dakota in the late 1930s.

dust pneumonia. Fish choked in mucky streams. Cows, rabbits, and birds collapsed in pastures, their lungs clogged with grit.

Even indoors, families could not escape the dust. They taped their window frames and waxed their doorsills, and still dust whistled through cracks, collecting on plates and sheets and picture frames, which crashed to the floor under the weight. The editor of the *Morton County Farmer* in Colorado reported:

> We can see nothing out our windows but dirt. Every time
> our teeth...come together, you feel dirt and taste it; haven't
> heard a thing for hours, my ears are full; can't smell, my
> nose is full; can't walk, my shoes are full but not of feet.

The ecological disaster emptied many rural counties. Unable to raise crops in a desert, about 3.5 million farmers left their fields during "the dirty thirties." Packing their belongings in rickety trucks, often abandoning their houses, most headed west. Nearly 300,000 reached

A Texas cotton-picking family looks for cotton to pick in September 1931.

A typical shacktown community in the San Joaquin Valley, California

*Okies drive through Amarillo,
Texas, in July 1941.*

California, where those lucky enough to find jobs replaced Mexicans as migrant laborers picking fruits and vegetables. Even though they came from many states, not just Oklahoma, locals called them "Okies."

According to historian Don Worster, "the ultimate meaning of the dust storms of the 1930s was that America as a whole, not just the plains, was badly out of balance with its natural environment." People loved to visit the national parks, but few citizens paid attention to the limits of the land.

A NEW DEAL

A take-charge president, Franklin Delano Roosevelt invested in conservation to heal the depression-ravaged economy—and the landscape. Elected for the first of four terms in 1932, FDR immediately tackled the problem of unemployment. He created the Civilian Conservation Corps (CCC) to put young men to work. Living in rural camps run with military discipline, CCC workers fought forest fires, made maps, dug lakes, and built parks. Youths earned room, board, and $30 a month—$25 of which the government sent home to their struggling families. Between 1933 and 1942, the CCC employed about three million Americans and planted more than two billion trees.

Ed Sincic signed up in 1934. After graduating from high school at 16, he couldn't find a job. He planned to go out "bumming." "I wasn't a hellraiser, but I could become one," he said. "The C's gave me something to do."

Like many in the corps, Sincic grew up in an urban area, on the outskirts of Detroit. To enter the CCC, he had to pass a physical. When the doctor told him two teeth needed fillings, he had them pulled instead and joined the CCC that same day.

The army managed the camps—usually separate camps for blacks and whites in those days of racial segregation—and the interior and agriculture departments supervised the projects. Stationed first in Hartwick Pines, Michigan, near the Huron National Forest, Sincic planted seedlings—white and Norway pines raised in a nursery. Every day, about a dozen men lined up side by side. To keep the crew in rough marching-band order, twine stretched between the guys on either end of the line, and each planter followed a vertical furrow

Civilian Conservation Corps (CCC) workers dig in the hot sun.

marked earlier by a tractor. They used dibbles, steel bars sharpened to a point. Sincic recalls the motion: Jab the dibble in, push forward, yank back, flip a seedling out of the sack in his back, plug it in, stomp it down. "We got so we could plant individually about 2,000 a day," he says.

Near Jellico, Tennessee, farm boy Ernie Taylor staffed a fire tower for the CCC, scanning wooded hillsides for the first telltale wisps of smoke. On another assignment, he and a partner identified trees, measuring the diameter of each trunk with a tape measure and recording it in a notebook. "You was walking through weeds and bushes up to

A CCC worker quarries rock in the 1930s.

African Americans were integrated into CCC camps in states where black recruits were too few in number to form separate camps.

your waist," said Taylor. Once he came down with such a bad case of poison ivy that the camp doctor almost performed surgery on the rash.

CCC crews exercised their muscles by day and stretched their minds by night. Camps offered classes—biology, math, photography. For most of the teens and men in their twenties, "CCC was just a job," said Damon Mackey. "I could send money back home." Conservation was secondary. "Back then, there wasn't any word put out that the environment was going bad," said Ernie Taylor.

Yet the men took pride in their work. "I thought we was doing the right thing," said Mackey. "Just about anything you could do was an improvement," added Ed Sincic. Many responsible youths, like Sincic, turned their CCC promotions into job offers from the Forest or the Soil Conservation Services. World War II ended almost all these conservation careers in the 1940s, as men got drafted into the military. But few CCC veterans forgot their wilderness experiences. In 1960, Sincic visited Hartwick Pines to stand under trees 30 to 40 feet tall that he had planted a quarter century before. The C's, he said, "gave you a respect for the area."

SOD BUILDERS

Roosevelt's New Deal policies also rushed to the rescue of farmers. Soil abuse had troubled a few farsighted Americans even before the Dust Bowl. George Washington Carver, born a slave in Missouri and later educated as an agricultural chemist, preached crop diversity. On the faculty at Tuskegee Institute from 1896 through the 1930s, he experimented with peanuts, sweet potatoes, and soybeans as alternatives to cotton and tobacco, which robbed more nutrients from the soil.

Another Southerner, Hugh Hammond Bennett, sounded the erosion alarm for years in the U.S. Department of Agriculture. In 1935, as dust from New Mexico clouded over Washington, D.C., Bennett took his concerns to Congress:

> Not mere soil is going down the slopes, down the rivers, down to the wastes of the oceans. Opportunity, security, the chance for a man to make a living from the land—these are going too.

Soon Bennett was heading the new Soil Conservation Service (SCS).

The SCS could not replace the land lost. Accumulating an inch of topsoil naturally takes from 300 to 1,000 years, Bennett said. To save what remained, the SCS promoted conservation techniques: contour tilling (plowing along the curves or contours of the land), listing (plowing up ridges of earth like corduroy fabric), residue management (leaving stubble in place after harvest), and letting fields lie fallow (or unused). Bennett wanted to allow native grasses to reclaim some pasture, and for awhile, the government paid farmers to plant them.

Most importantly, Bennett—known as Big Hugh or The Chief—communicated his message well. The SCS supported local soil conservation districts, neighbors teaching—and policing—each other. Soon green-and-white signs by the road marked these areas of cooperation.

Another FDR-era agency, the Tennessee Valley Authority (TVA), set

A dam under construction in the Tennessee Valley

an example of regional planning and local responsibility. The TVA planted forests, which helped halt the erosion plaguing the overfarmed Tennessee River valley. TVA dams controlled floods and provided cheap electricity. For poor communities along the Tennessee River basin, the TVA brought a chance to shed rural isolation.

"ONE HUMMING COMMUNITY"

In the 1930s and 1940s, Aldo Leopold, a professor of wildlife management at the University of Wisconsin, influenced a generation of students with his concept of biota—that every living creature belonged to "one humming community of cooperations and competitions." For decades, ranchers and government rangers had been trapping and poisoning predators they considered evil, such as wolves, while nurturing

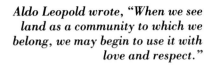

Aldo Leopold wrote, "When we see land as a community to which we belong, we may begin to use it with love and respect."

animals they considered innocent, such as deer. Leopold noticed, however, that without wolves to prey on them, mule deer on the Kaibab Plateau in Arizona multiplied out of control, stripping off the vegetation until many eventually starved to death. Leopold marveled at the checks and balances of the ecosystem. In his writings, he challenged people to practice a land ethic, to sacrifice for the greater good of the natural community.

Leopold belonged to a small and largely ignored group of intellectuals. In the Dust Bowl, for instance, farmers bristled at suggestions that challenged their way of life. They disliked experts who advised government to buy up marginal land and move families elsewhere. A presidential commission produced a report, *The Future of the Great Plains*, that criticized attitudes—the belief, for instance, that people can manipulate nature however they please.

Farmers weren't the only blind optimists. Throughout the dirty thirties, artists dramatized the Dust Bowl, but the public ignored the subtle protest in their art. Woody Guthrie sang "that dusty old dust is a-getting my home," and people hummed. Alexander Hogue painted a live rattlesnake beside dead cows in his eerie *Drouth Survivors* (1936). Critics liked the canvas; midwesterners hated it; almost no one considered it an environmental fable. Photographers Dorothea Lange and Arthur Rothstein documented hardship on the plains for the Farm Security Administration. In their photos, grimy children cling to worn women and dust buries sorry cabins of sod, but many viewers saw that devastation as temporary. After John Steinbeck chronicled the plight of Okies in *The Grapes of Wrath* (1939), he won a Pulitzer Prize. Although millions of Americans also saw the movie starring Henry Fonda, few took to heart Steinbeck's criticism of big agribusiness.

Those who stayed on the plains pulled through together. They shared grim jokes and disaster stories. And when better weather and World War II arrived in the early 1940s, they complained about conservation rules. They put every acre they could into wheat to earn a profit and to help the United States feed its soldiers and its allies.

Although less severe than in the 1930s, drought returned after World War II. Halfhearted soil conservation efforts couldn't prevent more dust storms in the filthy fifties.

Dorothea Lange photographed a roadside settlement in the San Joaquin Valley. The public believed that the drought and devastation in Lange's photographs and Steinbeck's writings were only temporary.

POLLUTING THE PLANET

If you visit American city,
You will find it very pretty.
Just two things of which you
*   must beware*
Don't drink the water and don't
*   breathe the air!*

Pollution, pollution
They've got smog and sewage
*   and mud.*
Turn on your tap,
And get hot and cold running
*   crud.*
  —songwriter Tom Lehrer,
        "Pollution," 1965

I n 1959, most Americans ate Thanksgiving turkey without the usual dollop of cranberry sauce. In early November, the Food and Drug Administration had recalled cranberries grown in Washington and Oregon that carried traces of the weed killer ATZ, aminotriazole. ATZ caused thyroid cancer in laboratory rats. Panicking, the public steered clear of canned sauce as well as fresh fruit.

In response, Ocean Spray Cranberry Company officials summoned television cameras to a press conference and munched the sour berries as if they were the sweetest grapes. Vice President Richard Nixon also served himself four helpings of cranberry sauce and lived to tell about it. Banning the use of ATZ on food crops probably did the most to reassure consumers. Within a few months, consumers welcomed cranberries back to their dinner tables.

The next scare wasn't resolved so quickly. Rachel Carson, a respected marine biologist and writer, touched off a fierce debate about pesticides with the publication of *Silent Spring* in 1962. Chemists had created more than 200 of these "elixirs of death" since the mid-1940s, she wrote, and many, such as dichloro-diphenyl-trichloroethane (DDT), entered the food chain. Birds, fish, and frogs ate tainted bugs—and they in turn got eaten. Carson warned:

> For the first time in the history of the world, every human being is now subjected to contact with dangerous chemicals, from the moment of conception until death.... They have

A tractor spreads pesticides on a field of corn.

Rachel Carson, above left, *a marine biologist, looks for snapping shrimp in her research along the Florida Keys.*

Rachel Carson uses a microscope to observe specimens collected from tidepools.

been found in fish in remote mountain lakes, in earthworms burrowing in soil, in the eggs of birds—and in man himself.

Meanwhile, pests were developing resistance to these toxins.

Conservationists applauded Carson's insight. Pesticide manufacturers, on the other hand, attacked her ideas even before they hit bookshelves. "Silent Spring Is Now a Noisy Summer," a headline reported after the *New Yorker* published excerpts from the book. In the early 1960s, the chemical industry was earning $250 million a year; it had a lot to lose. Leaning on friends in the media, it broadcast a blizzard of publicity in its defense—dealing some low blows to Carson. One company parodied *Silent Spring* in a pamphlet, "The Desolate Year," describing insects devouring their way to world rule. Another wrote to Carson's publisher and implied that she was slandering American business as part of a Communist plot.

Along with *Science* and *Reader's Digest*, *Time* magazine dismissed *Silent Spring* as an "emotional and inaccurate outburst." Many Americans found it hard to believe that chemists could have so miscalculated.

AGE OF AEROSOLS AND SARAN WRAP

In 1943, the military had begun powdering soldiers and refugees in Europe with DDT to kill the lice that spread deadly typhus. Two years later, the military had sprayed DDT on tropical mosquitoes that carried malaria. Like many innovations out of the laboratory, DDT had helped the Allies win World War II.

The war shaped a generation of Americans. Civilians practiced conservation—not to lessen the toll on nature, but to free up supplies for the military. Workers carpooled or rode buses to save gas. Parents and children recycled rubber, metal, even bacon fat. "Use it up, wear it out, make it do, or do without," one slogan urged. But after the Germans and then the Japanese surrendered in 1945, veterans and their families looked forward to a return to "normal life." They expected a reward for years of sacrifice—the chance to build a house, buy a couple of cars, and raise kids.

Many Americans lived out this dream in suburbs in the 1950s and 1960s. They didn't ask where the lumber for their sprawling ranch home was coming from or where the exhaust from their gas-guzzling Chevy was going. To meet demand for housing, developers piped water into deserts and dumped soil into marshes to create building lots. Pesticides, plastics, the atom bomb—all spawned peacetime industries. Americans of the 1950s thanked wartime technology for their steady jobs, their burping Tupperware, their bugless backyards. In a 1957 poll, 90 percent said the world was "better off because of science."

Yet a vocal minority of citizens continued to press for environmental protection. Bill Partington, a storekeeper who studied frogs and snakes as a hobby, moved to Florida in the 1960s to direct a nature center. With other conservationists, he urged the state to stop dredging and filling wetlands that served as filters for water and nurseries for fish and birds:

> A lot of people thought we were absolutely nuts. Here was all this yucky landscape that nobody wanted...and obviously the sensible stuff was to pump it up and make waterfront property with seawalls and lawns and houses and drive-ways.... That was the sensible thing. That made money for people. It made for "clean living." Maybe you were polluting the daylights out of that waterway in front of you, but...your lawn was clean.

New environmental groups were forming. Professional ecologists founded the Nature Conservancy in 1951 to buy land to preserve. Long-established groups were widening their concerns. As the National Audubon Society realized, protecting the bald eagle meant protecting its habitat, from rivers where the birds drank to forests where they nested.

By 1950, the Sierra Club numbered 7,000 members. It soon hired its first professional staff—just in time for a battle. Two federal agencies were building cash register dams all over the arid West. Water power generated electricity, which officials sold at a profit to fund irrigation. Growing cities and suburbs made some of these projects necessary, but the Sierra Club drew the line when the Bureau of Reclamation proposed damming the Green River at a place called Echo Park within Dinosaur National Monument.

To prevent another ruined canyon like Hetch Hetchy, the Sierra Club mounted a massive public-relations campaign. It took out ads in newspapers. Volunteers led float trips down the river for journalists, politicians, and vacationers. When *Collier's* magazine presented pro-and-con viewpoints, it included a letter from nine-year-old Kim Bradley:

> Dear President Eisenhower,
>
> Please don't build a dam in Dinosaur Park. It is beautiful and exciting and fun riding on rubber rafts on the huge waves.
>
> I went there once and want to go again. If you had been down it, you would not build a dam.

For anyone who couldn't ride the rapids in Colorado, the Sierra Club produced a film and published a book. In Washington, D.C., the head of the Sierra Club testified before Congress and pointed out mistakes in the planners' calculations. Assorted conservation groups presented a united opposition and produced letters from voters who supported them. Legislators listened. In 1955, the Bureau of Reclamation scrapped the Echo Park dam.

The hullabaloo over *Silent Spring* reached even farther than the publicity over Echo Park. Rachel Carson made sense to many ordinary Americans. They too had doubts about how people were using scientific discoveries, about new chemicals and atomic power. Although citizens had welcomed the bomb as a superweapon in 1945 to speed the end of World War II, the arms race between the United States and the Soviet Union had frayed their nerves. As kids practiced duck-and-cover at school and adults studied plans for fallout shelters in case of nuclear war, they began to wonder: Was it wise to unleash a force that could blow up the entire planet? Aboveground nuclear tests in the 1950s also released strontium-90, a radioactive element that scattered all over the globe. From soil to grass to cow, strontium-90 entered the

Aboveground nuclear tests — like this atomic blast at Bikini Island on July 25, 1946 — release harmful radioactive particles into the atmosphere.

milk supply and settled, like calcium, in bones. Parents feared children would develop bone cancer and leukemia.

Many concerned viewers tuned in to a CBS-TV special in 1963 that featured a chemical-industry representative, government officials, and Rachel Carson. Even though she was dying of breast cancer, the shy 55-year-old writer quietly and forcefully made her case. She wasn't a crackpot; she was a scientist questioning the ethics of her profession. As she wrote so poetically in *Silent Spring*, humans shouldn't assume that they can control the fabric of life—"a fabric on the one hand delicate and destructible, on the other miraculously tough and resilient, capable of striking back in unexpected ways." Like Aldo Leopold, she argued that people should accommodate, not dominate, nature.

After the show, letters swamped CBS—and Washington. President Kennedy's Science Advisory Committee was already investigating the issue. A few months later, it reached the same conclusion Carson had, that people needed to use and to monitor pesticides more carefully. Even *Time* changed its stance and acknowledged Carson's foresight. In 1969, the United States finally began banning DDT.

"THE TIMES, THEY ARE A-CHANGIN' "

Silent Spring marked a watershed in environmental awareness, a wake-up call for the public after two decades of indifference. It added momentum to the grass-roots movement in the 1960s. Even folks who didn't read very much watched television, which proved to be a powerful ally of conservationists. From their Lazyboy loungers, Americans could visit national parks without getting a mosquito bite. Nature programming was popular, thanks in part to color television sets and the magic of time-lapse photography. Weekly shows like *Wild Kingdom* (1963-1988), hosted by zoo director Marlin Perkins, educated families in their living rooms.

In 1964, with public interest in wildlife running high, Congress finally approved the Wilderness Bill, which set aside areas "where the earth and its community of life are untrammeled by man, where man himself is a visitor who does not remain." Next, lawmakers passed a series of increasingly strict Endangered Species acts in 1966, 1969, and 1973.

Television also brought home disturbing images of pollution—smog over Los Angeles, gunk in the Great Lakes. President Lyndon Johnson's wife, Lady Bird, led a popular national campaign to beautify the United States. She took particular interest in planting wildflowers along highways. But, as the decade wore on, beautification struck more and more Americans, especially young people, as a superficial response to the poisoning of the environment.

Outrage was simmering among baby boomers—the huge generation born to the veterans of World War II. Although teachers and parents had promised a future full of happiness and ease, boomers were discovering flaws in American society during the turbulent 1960s. Police sicked dogs on African Americans protesting peacefully for equal opportunities. As consumer advocate Ralph Nader revealed in his expose about poorly made cars, *Unsafe at Any Speed* (1965), big business often endangered the public in its rush for profits. Most disturbing of all, the United States was mired in a savage civil war in Vietnam. As TV journalists revealed through their war zone coverage, young Americans were losing their lives or their limbs or their innocence in the jungle. Why?

The answers of the Establishment—the white men who ran most of government and business—did not satisfy the baby boomers. As evidence mounted that U.S. officials were mismanaging the war, disillusioned citizens began to wonder: Maybe the kids were right to question authority. The ugly failures of business and government appeared on television. In January 1969, oil leaked from under a Union Oil Company drilling platform off California, blackening the beaches of Santa Barbara and coating water birds with deadly slime. Then the news cameras turned on the Cuyahoga River near Cleveland, Ohio, so polluted with grease and trash that it spontaneously caught fire.

Two U.S. senators inspect the harbor at Santa Barbara as the oil leak from an offshore drilling platform saturates the area's beaches and harbors with oil.

Poet Archibald MacLeish called the Earth — shown here from Apollo 11 *in July 1969 — "that bright loveliness in the eternal cold."*

One image from that troubled year put the ecological crisis in perspective. As the Apollo 10 spacecraft rocketed toward the moon in May 1969 with a color TV camera in its cabin, the crew sent back the first photograph of the entire Earth. Shimmering with blue oceans and swirled in white clouds, the planet hung against the black backdrop of space like a beautiful, delicate ornament. *Life* magazine reported: "80 million Earthlings watched their world shrink." One writer in *Look* magazine explained:

> Suddenly, we could understand what [politician and diplomat] Adlai Stevenson had said: "We travel together, passengers on a little spaceship; dependent on its vulnerable reserves of air and soil; all committed for our safety to its security and peace; preserved from annihilation only by the care, the work, and...the love we give our fragile craft."

The image gave new meaning to the metaphor of Spaceship Earth.

In July 1969, a global audience watched U.S. astronaut Neil Armstrong take a giant leap for humankind by stepping on to the moon. People of all ages and all nationalities posed the logical next question: If we could send a man to the moon, why couldn't we clean up our act on Earth?

MAKING "GREEN" ROUTINE

Think globally, act locally.
  —environmental slogan,
     1970s–1980s

Earth Day 1970: In Seattle, students held a "trash-in," carting garbage to the companies that produced it. In Atlanta, they piled up no-return bottles in front of Coca-Cola headquarters. In Knoxville, they skimmed swill from the Tennessee River. Roughly 12,000 school and college campuses held events or workshops about the environment.

Organizing the protest from a cramped office in Washington, D.C., the youthful leaders of Environmental Action Inc. aimed at nothing less than revolution. "We will feel Earth Day has failed if it stops at pollution, if it doesn't serve as a catalyst in the values of society," coordinator Denis Hayes told *Newsweek* magazine.

Few others took Earth Day so seriously. Despite symbolic car bashings and mock funerals with coffins full of trash, Earth Day lacked the angry edge of anti-war marches. New York City closed Fifth Avenue to cars for two hours, and 100,000 pedestrians strolled in the April sunshine. NBC news crews rode horse-drawn buggies.

Politicians, labor leaders, and business executives did use Earth Day to try to narrow the generation gap. Congress recessed, and 22 senators attended teach-ins around the country. Scott Paper Company

Opposite: *Earth Day is in full swing in Manhattan's Union Square Park.*
Above: *Fifth Avenue is filled with thousands of people at noon on Earth Day,*
April 22, 1970.

announced a $36 million pollution-control program. The governors of
New York and New Jersey created state environmental agencies. But,
as *Newsweek* asked in a headline, was Earth Day "a giant step or a
springtime skip?" Journalists around the country noted that the secretary of the interior approved a controversial oil pipeline through 800
miles of pristine Alaska wilderness. That day, four U.S. car makers
rolled 35,000 new sources of exhaust off the assembly line. "The
Establishment sees this as a great big anti-litter campaign," complained California representative George Brown. "Most Establishment
people don't have any idea what it would mean to their lifestyle to
clean up the Earth."

Even so, the widespread participation in Earth Day indicated a shift
in attitudes. Membership in environmental groups tripled in the following year. Politicians responded. Starting with the National
Environmental Protection Act (NEPA) of 1970, Congress enacted a
series of laws to improve air and water quality.

NEPA set up the Environmental Protection Agency (EPA) to conduct research and set standards. It also authorized citizens to sue both government agencies and private industries when they failed to comply. Many of the new conservation groups in the 1970s—such as the Sierra Club Legal Defense Fund—made their cases in court.

As an officer of the Florida Audubon Society, Bill Partington noticed that change was trickling down to the state level:

> We were always being ridiculed as these birdwatchers.... But by and large [state leaders] started to see this thing was a growing movement, and it was national, too. So that was a good time for all of us. Nationally, there were a lot of guilt-ridden outfits, foundations, and charities...that had always been real destroyers of the environment...like the Ford Foundation, from whom I got a grant. All of a sudden they were turning around and looking for good causes to put money into to prove they weren't such terrible people after all. That was the tone of the time.

"ONCE IS NOT ENOUGH—RECYCLE"

Environmental sensitivity extended beyond new laws. Even if the Establishment didn't believe that conservation required a simpler lifestyle, many baby boomers did. In the late 1960s and early 1970s, the youthful counterculture recycled old ideas about nature, quoting Thoreau's *Walden* and Native American sayings. Like Thoreau, a few headed back to the land to farm—not alone, but in groups called communes. In 1969, *Life* visited one such commune, where 41 people, including 11 children, were living in tepees "somewhere out in the woods." They called themselves The Family. While men split logs for the cast-iron stove, women harvested beans and squash. "Getting out of the cities isn't hard, only concrete is," read part of The Family's creed. "Plant a garden, find a center."

Even people who didn't join communes browsed through *The Whole Earth Catalog* (1968), a guide to environmentally friendly tools and products such as solar water heaters. Nutrition gurus were preaching about health—and about agriculture's toll on the environment. Frances Moore Lappe, a social worker who dropped out of graduate school, wrote about the wastefulness of raising meat in *Diet for a Small Planet* (1971). To produce 1 pound of beef, farmers feed cattle 16 pounds of grains and soybeans that humans might otherwise eat.

The average steak-loving American considered these ideas far-out. But baby boomers set trends. American Indian themes surfaced in beaded clothes and movies like *Billy Jack* (1973). Keep America Beautiful, an anti-litter group, sponsored memorable public-service ads on television, featuring Iron Eyes Cody, a Cherokee actor. In one spot, he paddled down a river full of litter, beached his canoe, then climbed up a bank to a highway. As a car whizzed by, someone tossed out a bag of trash that split open at his feet. A single tear rolled down the Indian's cheek. "People start pollution," said the voice-over. "People can stop it."

The pesticide scare—and government warnings about mercury found in tuna and swordfish—brought customers to new health-food shops. Granola helped account for $3 billion in sales in 1970. *The Last Whole Earth Catalog* (1971), with a photo of Spaceship Earth on the cover, sold hundreds of thousands of copies and won a National

Iron Eyes Cody sheds a tear for the environment.

Book Award. While hippies plastered bumper stickers on their Volkswagen vans—"Save Water, Shower with a Friend" or "Preserve Democracy: Seal It in Plastic"—even suburban station wagons sometimes sported "Real People Wear Fake Furs" or "Ecology Now!"

Riding a wave of public interest, environmental groups wondered if "the greening of America" was a fad or a true change of heart. The energy crisis of the 1970s tested the public's willingness to sacrifice in order to save natural resources.

In 1973, Americans accounted for 6 percent of the world's population and consumed more than 30 percent of the world's fuel. A war in the Middle East led to an oil shortage that forced the United States to confront its disorganized energy policy. Many of the plans to generate power from different sources posed pollution risks. Burning coal contributed to acid rain and smog. Nuclear plants produced radioactive waste. Drilling for oil off the coast of the United States endangered coral reefs and wetlands.

When President Jimmy Carter took office in 1977, he urged fuel conservation. Setting an example by turning down the thermostat and wearing a sweater during a televised chat, the president called upon citizens to unite in an effort that was "the moral equivalent of war."

Although Americans had carpooled and shivered cheerfully through World War II, they didn't respond to the moral equivalent of war. They had grown more dependent on the comfort and convenience of automobiles. By 1970, 80 percent of American households owned at least one car and used it daily. Demand for energy remained high, and drivers resented high prices and long lines for gas. Displeasure with the hardships of the Carter years contributed to the 1980 landslide victory of Ronald Reagan, a pro-business Republican opposed by most environmental groups.

BELOW THE SURFACE

Reagan's appointment of James Watt as secretary of the interior confirmed the worst fears of environmentalists. A Wyoming-born lawyer with ties to logging, mining, and real-estate interests in the West, Watt

The scars from strip mining at Bingham Canyon, Utah, contrast with the snowcapped mountains in the background. Each step is 40 to 70 feet high.

admitted having "a bias for private enterprise." He halted the purchase of parklands, eased rules for strip miners, and opened the oceans' outer continental shelf to oil exploration. He also attacked nature advocates like the Sierra Club as liberal and elitist.

Environmental groups fought back by turning the media spotlight on Watt's insensitive remarks. Ed Stein, editorial cartoonist for the *Rocky Mountain News*, frequently mocked federal environmental policy, which he summed up in this takeoff of "America, the Beautiful":

> Oh, beautiful! Our federal lands
> on sale for waves of green.
> Want a purple mountain majesty?
> That'll be a buck-nineteen!
> America, America,
> Here's what they plan for thee.
> To rape thy land for cash in hand
> from sea to shining sea.

The lack of government support didn't halt grassroots environmental efforts. In fact, the Sierra Club attracted new followers. Between 1980 and 1988, it more than doubled in size, from 182,000 to 440,000 members. When the Exxon tanker *Valdez* spilled 11 million gallons of crude oil into Alaska's Prince William Sound in May 1989, 27,000 Americans joined the Wilderness Society.

Historians dubbed the 1980s the decade of greed. But it was also a decade of quiet alarm. As the rich got richer, many other Americans got worried. Back in 1968, *Time* magazine assured readers that "just as technology has polluted the country, it can also depollute it." Over

In the port of Valdez, workers mop up oil tracked in on fishing boats slimed by their passage through Prince William Sound.

The crippled oil tanker Exxon Valdez *is escorted into San Diego Bay on July 30, 1989, by a flotilla of environmentalists after the tanker finally received permission to enter state waters for a $25 million repair.*

the next two decades, people discovered that technology could not always correct mistakes.

Nuclear accidents—first at the Three Mile Island power plant in Pennsylvania, then more seriously at the Chernobyl plant in the Soviet Union—released radioactive gases into the atmosphere. After children in Love Canal, New York, developed unusually high rates of cancers, residents learned their homes had been built on a chemical dump site. In 1980, the EPA had to relocate 2,500 people and burn down 237 houses and a school.

Toxic waste turned up all over the country in the 1980s. It turned up in Times Beach, Missouri, because town leaders had sprayed oil contaminated with poisonous dioxin to keep dust down. It turned up in many poor neighborhoods, along with a high rate of illness. One stretch of Louisiana near petrochemical plants earned the nickname Cancer Alley. The frustrating search for answers and help turned ordinary people into activists. Steve Curwood, a radio journalist, noted that African Americans were awakening to environmental problems:

> Earth Day 1970 was a largely white thing; the ecology movement of the 1970s often meant rich people practicing conservation. But now you see Jesse Jackson leading a "toxic tour" of the South. Three of the five largest toxic-waste dumps in the country are in minority communities.

Concerned citizens wanted to do more than write checks to eco-groups. Many followed the suggestions in *Simple Things You Can Do to Save the Earth* (1989), such as turning off the faucet while they brushed their teeth. Very slowly, a revolution in lifestyle was taking hold.

In 1986, Linda Maraniss was walking along a beach in Texas when she spotted a young mother settling down on a blanket to nurse her baby. "She made a clean spot for herself by pushing away the trash," Maraniss recalls.

> That image really upset me.... I grew up in Wisconsin, and every November, my dad would drive my family all the way to Florida—three days in the station wagon, three kids eating sandwiches out of a cooler. And as we got closer, we'd start peeling off our clothes. By the time we got to Daytona Beach, we'd be taking off our shoes, and then we'd get there and put our bare feet in the warm sand. And it was heaven. So I got the idea the beach was a special place.

Maraniss, an educator with the Center for Marine Conservation, decided to do something. She organized volunteers to pick up debris on the shore. Girl Scouts, retirees, families, teachers, managers—all signed on as "beach buddies." Everyone carried a card to record what had washed up: diapers, egg cartons, syringes, and plastic six-pack rings (that can strangle pelicans).

The annual cleanup grew. Armed with the information collected, conservationists shamed the navy into using trash compactors. They prodded plastics manufacturers to encourage recycling. They convinced Congress to outlaw ocean dumping. In 1992, more than

145,000 people in 33 states and 12 foreign countries scoured 4,290 miles of beach. "It shows how powerful people are when they work together," Maraniss says.

"DON'T STOP THINKING ABOUT TOMORROW"

Economics steered more and more Americans toward environmentally sound practices by the end of the 1980s. Cleaning up cost a fortune. For the *Valdez* spill alone, Exxon paid more than $2 billion. Prevention, on the other hand, often saved money. Recycling aluminum, paper, plastics, and glass was cheaper than incineration or landfill space. Companies also discovered that they could win new "green" customers, or keep old ones, by reducing packaging and fighting pollution.

People are recycling their glass, cans, and papers all over the country.

As always, conservation groups had different priorities and different tactics. Some bought land. Some wrote letters to Congress. Others, like members of Greenpeace, staged daring protests, such as sailing into nuclear test zones. Some radical believers in deep ecology embraced sabotage, or ecotage. Earth First! vowed "no compromise in defense of Mother Earth." To halt logging in old-growth forests, Earth First! punctured tires, burned bulldozers, and drove spikes into trunks. Although the big nails didn't hurt the trees, they could damage expensive saws—and possibly injure loggers.

Most people disapproved of such extreme tactics. Even more moderate efforts to protect wilderness stirred conflict—at times with landowners defending their property rights or with workers fighting for their jobs. Environmentalism often meant trading the present profit of a few people for the future benefit of many. Yet according to a 1990 poll, 74 percent of Americans agreed that "protecting the environment is so important that requirements and standards cannot be too high, and continuing environmental improvements must be made regardless of cost."

Although the roots of conservation date back to the 19th century, only at the end of the 20th century had it really begun to bloom. As the gathering of world leaders at the 1990 Earth Summit in Brazil demonstrated, the environment had become an international concern, not just an American one. Pollution respects no borders. Spaceship Earth depends on the great variety of the planet's ecosystems to survive.

Retiree Walt Love marvels at the turnaround within his lifetime. As a teenager mining coal in Pennsylvania in the 1930s, he paid little attention to the slag and sulfur his company was pouring into creeks. "We had lots of fresh water," he says. "What did we worry about them ruining one creek?"

Love served in the CCC, protecting wildlife and curbing erosion. Still, he didn't blame any business for trying to exploit natural resources. After World War II, he worked in a steel mill for 27 years. "They would dump chemicals on the ground. But I don't think anybody was worrying. You figured there would be no end. You only worried about the environment around you. A five to ten mile trip— that was as far as you ever went."

When Love retired, he moved more than 1,000 miles to Florida. There he opens his morning paper and reads stories from across the country and around the globe about people struggling to save rivers and rain forests and endangered rhinoceroses. "Right now you don't live in a small community anymore," Walter Love says. "You live in the world."

Ansel Adams took this photo of Grand Canyon National Park, Arizona, in 1941. With good conservation practices, the Grand Canyon will be preserved for hundreds of years.

BIBLIOGRAPHY

Anderson, Bruce N. *Ecologue: The Environmental Catalogue and Consumer's Guide for a Safe Earth.* New York: Prentice Hall, 1990.

Bergon, Frank, and Zeese Papanikolas, eds. *Looking Far West: The Search for the American West in History, Myth, and Literature.* New York: New American Library, 1978.

Busch, Noel F. *TR: The Story of Theodore Roosevelt and his Influence on Our Times.* New York: Reynal, 1963.

Carson, Rachel. *Silent Spring.* Boston: Houghton Mifflin, 1962.

Clement, Fred. *Department of the Interior.* New York: Chelsea House, 1989.

Cronon, William. *Changes in the Land: Indians, Colonists, and the Ecology of New England.* New York: Hill and Wang, 1983.

Dickson, Paul. *Timelines.* Reading, Mass.: Wesley Publishing, 1990.

Dunlap, Thomas R. *Saving America's Wildlife.* Princeton, N.J.: Princeton Univ. Press, 1988.

Everhart, William C. *The National Park Service.* Boulder, Colo.: Westview Press, 1983.

Goetzmann, William H. *Exploration and Empire: The Explorer and the Scientist in the Winning of the American West.* New York: W. W. Norton, 1966.

Goetzmann, William H., and William N. Goetzmann. *The West of the Imagination.* New York: W. W. Norton, 1986.

Graham, Frank, Jr. *Man's Dominion: The Story of Conservation in America.* New York: M. Evans, 1971.

Hynes, H. Patricia. *Earth Right.* Rocklin, Calif.: Prima Publishing, 1990.

Jezer, Marty. *Rachel Carson.* New York: Chelsea House, 1988.

Manes, Christopher. *Green Rage: Radical Environmentalism and the Unmaking of Civilization.* Boston: Little, Brown, 1990.

Martin, Cy. *The Saga of the Buffalo.* New York: Hart Publishing, 1973.

McAdams, Cliff. *Yellowstone National Park Guide and Reference Book.* Boulder, Colo.: Preutt Publishing, 1981.

McHenry, Robert, with Charles van Doren, ed. *A Documentary History of Conservation in America.* New York: Praeger Publishers, 1972.

Nash, Roderick, ed. *The American Environment: Readings in the History of Conservation.* Reading, Mass.: Addison-Wesley, 1968.

——. *The Call of the Wild (1900-1916).* New York: George Braziller, 1970.

O'Neil, Doris, ed. *LIFE in the '60s.* Boston: Little, Brown, 1989.

Piller, Charles. *The Fail-Safe Society.* New York: Basic Books, 1991.

Teale, Edwin Way, ed. *The Wilderness World of John Muir.* Boston: Houghton Mifflin, 1954.

Thoreau, Henry David. *Walden and Other Writings.* New York: Modern Library, 1950.

Trefethen, James B. *An American Crusade for Wildlife.* New York: Winchester Press, 1975.

Turner, Tom. *Sierra Club: 100 Years of Protecting Nature.* New York: Abrams, 1991.

Wadsworth, Ginger. *John Muir: Wilderness Protector.* Minneapolis: Lerner Publications, 1992.

——. *Rachel Carson: Voice for the Earth.* Minneapolis: Lerner Publications, 1992.

Wilson, R. L. *Theodore Roosevelt Outdoorsman.* New York: Winchester Press, 1971.

Worster, David. *Dust Bowl: The Southern Plains in the 1930s.* New York: Oxford Univ. Press, 1979.

INDEX

abundance of natural resources, 13-14, 16, 18-21
Adams, Ansel, 83
atom bomb. *See* radioactive contamination
Audubon, John James, 32
Audubon Society, 66, 74

Baden-Powell, Robert, 42-43
Bennett, Hugh Hammond, 58
Bierstadt, Albert, 16, 33, 41
biota. *See* ecology
birds, 13, 23-25, 37, 66, 70. *See also* endangered species; extinction of species
bison, 18-23. *See also* endangered species; extinction of species
Bloomer, Amelia Jenks, 42
Boy Scouts, 42-43
Bryce Canyon, 45
business use of natural resources, 20-23, 30-31, 32, 37-39, 49, 60-61, 65, 69-70, 73, 76-77, 78, 81, 82-83

campaigning for national parks. *See* national parks
cancer, 68, 79-80
Carson, Rachel, 63-65, 67, 68-69
Carver, George Washington, 58
chemicals. *See* pesticides; pollution; radioactive contamination
Civilian Conservation Corps (CCC), 54-58, 82
Cleveland National Forest, 46
Cody, Buffalo Bill, 21-22, 41
Colorado River, 26, 28, 36
Colter, John, 7

conservation ethic. *See* environmentalism
conservation: to heal exploited land, 54-59, 80-81, 82-83; of land for its own sake, 29-31, 37, 41-42, 48, 66, 69, 82; of land as natural resource, 28, 34, 37, 38-39, 47-49, 54-59; of natural resources, 35, 65, 66-67, 71, 76, 80-81; of wildlife for hunting, 32-33, 35, 37. *See also* preservation

Darwin, 25
DDT. *See* pesticides
de Tocqueville, Alexis, 15-16
Douglas, William O., 65
drought, 28, 61. *See also* Dust Bowl
Dust Bowl, 50-54, 58, 60-61

Earth Day, 72-73, 80
Earth First!, 82
ecology, 26, 59-60, 68, 71, 82-83
ecotage, 82
endangered species, 23-25, 37, 41, 66, 69, 83
environmentalism, 12, 17, 25, 33, 37, 47, 66, 69, 72-83
expansion, westward. *See* westward expansion
exploitation of natural resources, 14-16, 21-25, 30-31, 41, 50-51, 54, 60-61, 66, 75, 76-77, 82
extinction of species, 13, 18-19, 23-25
Exxon Valdez, 78, 79, 81

Forbes, Stephen A., 26
Fresh Air Fund, 42
frontier. *See* westward expansion

Girl Scouts (formerly Girl Guides), 43-44, 80-81
Grand Canyon, 26, 36, 37, 83
Great Depression, 49-50, 52-54
Greenpeace, 79, 82
Guthrie, Woody, 50, 60-61

Hayden, Ferdinand, 8-10, 13
Hetch Hetchy, 47-49, 67
hunting: as sport, 20-21, 32-33, 34, 35-36; for livelihood, 21-22, 23, 31, 32

industrialization, 18-19, 31-32, 41
industry. *See* business use of natural resources

Jackson, William Henry, 8-9, 10, 11
Johnson, Lady Bird, 69

Keep America Beautiful, 75
Knowles, Joseph, 42

land: as natural resource. *See* conservation; as natural wonder. *See* preservation
Lange, Dorothea, 53, 61
Lappe, Frances Moore, 75
Leopold, Aldo, 59-60, 68
Louisiana Purchase, 13
Low, Juliette "Daisy" Gordon, 43

Manifest Destiny. *See* westward expansion
Mather, Stephen, 44, 46
Moran, Thomas, 8-9, 10
Muir, John, 29-31, 35, 37, 40, 41-42, 48

national parks, 6, 7-8, 10-11, 12, 17, 31, 39, 42-49, 54
National Park Service, 46
Native American: lifestyles, 19-20, 22-23; views of the land, 7, 14, 18, 19-20, 74, 75
natural resources. *See under* abundance of natural resources; conservation; exploitation of natural resources
Nature Conservancy, 66
Niagara Falls, 12-13

oil spill, 70, 78, 79
Old Faithful, 6, 7, 10
outdoor recreation, 39-40, 41-47, 67

passenger pigeon. *See* birds
pesticides, 62-63, 65, 66, 67, 68-69, 75
Pinchot, Gifford, 37-39, 48-49
pollution, 62-63, 65-66, 69, 70, 72, 73-74, 75, 78-79, 82-83
Powell, John Wesley, 26-28, 37
preservation: of land as natural wonder, 6, 7, 11, 12, 16-17, 39. *See also* conservation
"progress," 15-16, 18-19, 20, 25

radioactive contamination, 66, 67-68, 76, 79
railroad, 16, 18, 20-21
recreation. *See* outdoor recreation
recycling, 74, 80, 81

regulated use of land. *See* conservation: of land as natural resource
Richards, Ellen Swallow, 26
Rocky Mountains, 16
Roosevelt, Franklin Delano, 54
Roosevelt, Theodore, 32-33, 34-35, 37, 39-40, 41, 47

Sequoia National Park, 47
Sierra Club, 42, 48, 66-67, 74, 77, 78
Sierra Nevada, 16-17, 29
soil conservation. *See* conservation: of natural resources
"Spaceship Earth," 71, 82, 83
Steinbeck, John, 61
surveys of United States, land, 7, 8-10, 13, 26-28

Tennessee Valley Authority (TVA), 58-59
Thoreau, Henry David, 29, 74
transcontinental railroad. *See* railroad
Turner, Frederick Jackson, 40-41

U.S. Geological Survey, 8, 26
U.S. Government agencies, 26, 38-39, 54-58, 73-74

Washburn, Henry, 7, 10
waste of natural resources. *See* exploitation of natural resources
water conservation. *See* conservation: of natural resources
Watt, James, 76-77
westward expansion, 15-16, 19, 20-21, 28, 41

wilderness, as antidote for civilization's ills, 29, 32, 39-40, 41-47

Yellowstone, 6-13, 16-17, 44
Yosemite, 13, 17, 29-31, 40, 42, 47-49

PHOTO ACKNOWLEDGMENTS

Photographs and illustrations reproduced with the permission of: National Archives, pp. 2 (#Am Im 30), 8 (#Am Im 26), 9 (#Am Im 208), 11 (#57-HS-78), 27 (#57-PS-77), 28 (#57-PS-444), 30 (#Am Im 209), 36 (#Am Im 207), 45 (#208-LU-32H-1), 46 (#Am Im 115), 50 (#Am Im 133), 51 (#Am Im 218), 52 (#114-DL-SD-5000), 53 (top #Am Im 126 and bottom #Am Im 146), 54 (#Am Im 147), 57 (#35-SU-1G-15), 61 (#Am Im 228), 62 (#412-G-6-48), 68 (#Am Im 181), 83 (#79-AAF-3), 88 (#171-G-10H-82619); Yellowstone National Park Collection, p. 6; Library of Congress, pp. 10, 17, 20, 21, 33, 34, 38, 43, 44, 47, 55, 56, 59; Ontario Archives, p. 12; Kansas State Historical Society, p. 15; Glenbow Photograph, p. 18; Smithsonian Institution, pp. 19 (#43, 118-A), 22 (#56, 630); Independent Picture Service, p. 24; California State Library, p. 31; Yosemite National Park Research Library, p. 35; Theodore Roosevelt Collection, Harvard College Library, p. 40; Colby Memorial Library, Sierra Club, pp. 48, 49; The Wilderness Society, p. 60; Agricultural Extension, University of Minnesota, p. 63; U.S. Fish and Wildlife/Rex Gary Schmidt, p. 64 (top); Beinecke Rare Book and Manuscript Library, Yale University, p. 64 (bottom); UPI/Bettmann, p. 70; NASA, p. 71; UPI/Bettmann Newsphotos, pp. 72, 73, 79; Keep America Beautiful, p. 75; Salt Lake Convention and Visitors Bureau, p. 77; Reuters/Bettmann Newsphotos, p. 78; Dawn M. Miller, p. 81.

Front and back cover painting: *The Grand Canyon of the Yellowstone* (detail) by Thomas Moran, reproduced with the permission of the National Museum of American Art, Smithsonian Institution, lent by the U.S. Department of the Interior, Office of the Secretary. Front cover photo by Arthur Rothstein, courtesy of the Library of Congress. Flag photo by IPS/Kathy Raskob.